EVERYDAY OBJECTS
CHANCE RE

DEREK ADAMS

To Jo

best wishes

Derek Adams

Southend '12

THE LITTORAL PRESS

First Published 2005

The Littoral Press
38 Barringtons, 10 Sutton Road,
Southend-on-Sea, Essex SS2 5NA

© 2005 Derek Adams

The right of Derek Adams to be identified as author
Of this work has been asserted by him under
The Copyright Designs and Patents Act 1988

British Library Cataloguing-in-Publication Data:
A catalogue record of this book is available from
The British Library

ISBN 09541844-7-5

Printed by 4edge Ltd. Hockley, Essex.

Keep your muse slender, your lines melodic and your thought compressed: leave thundering for Zeus.

Callimachus

Knowing things sometimes impedes the power of true observation. Those who see with their own eyes are truly fortunate.

Hamada

For my wife, Dolly, whose love and encouragement, daily help me climb this giant beanstalk to the clouds.
And for Jak who first showed me the magic beans.

Acknowledgements

Acknowledgements are due to the editors of the following publications in which some of these poems were first published:
Apostrophe, Clean Sheets, Dream People, Krax, Legend, Littoral, Moonstone, Obsessed with Pipework, Poetry Monthly, Poetry Nottingham, Read the Music, The Sensitively Thin Bill of the Shag (Biscuit Publishing, 2003), Sol, Southend Poetry, SpinDrifter, Strange Horizons, Uno (Comrades press 2002), Writer's Muse.

CONTENTS

TURNING POINT

In my secret sometimes world, where
once dreams ride a roundabout,
astride the painted wooden horse
whose hooves are forever springtime.

Where hands and lips that once were mine
revisit and re-run the course
and whisper what they used to shout:
that lovers do not dream, but dare

to walk with moonlight on their hair
(while others think the sun is out)
and call not once the name remorse,
for truth of heart must be no crime.

So take the leap, life holds the rein.
Chance unsaddled won't pass again.

SOFT LIKE FIRE

Like the mountains ahead
    you suture away

        the veins of memory
through dreams –

        brave martyrs stand;
            in the field, grass decays.

Martyrs rapture
        spreads like blood,

wax veins chain the
            heart's ancient rhythm,

soft like fire and complete
        beyond brief petal's deceit.

TECTONICS'

I sense a shift
beneath the surface,
a tension
in the constant
pushing and shoving
of emotional forces.

I scan your irises,
monitoring the subtle brown/green
colour shift, for signals
of the impending eruption;
that will send plates
crashing and colliding
against the kitchen wall.

CUT UP

The saw blade moves
rhythmically.
Back and forth.
Back and forth.

The saw teeth bite
alternately.
This way, then that.
This way, then that.

Pushing and stabbing.
Pulling and tearing.
To-ing and fro-ing.
Sawing and bowing.

The final bow
Separates.
Last pull
tears
and tears.

YOUR ABSENCE IS A WOUND

Your absence is a wound,
easily re-opened.
Everyday objects
and chance remarks
develop a cutting edge.

The familiar comes uninvited,
a ghost that refuses to appear
merely disturbs the atmosphere
with its silence –
taunting, flaunting,
echoing between my ears,

Your absence is a wound,
easily re-opened.
Teeth gritted, I slice old scars.
Watch: numb, expectant.
Emotions spatter.

FREE WORDS

Free words here, free words here.
Come and get your free words here.

Free words here, free words here.
No purchase necessary, nothing to pay,
Special offer: hear free words today.

Free words here, free words here.
Come and get your free words here.

Step up, come closer, draw near.
Do not fear, the only catch is in your ear.
Free words here, hear free words here.

Free words, free lines.
Free verse, free rhymes.
Free rein, free spirit.
Free kick, free trial.
Free love, free style.
Free speech, free lives.
Free offer, free inside.
Free the Jackson five.

Free one, free all.
Free base, free fall.
Free agent, free hand.
Free range, free land.
Free house, free nation
Free Church, freemason
Free association.

Freeway, freewheel.
Free man, Free voice.
Free slave, free will.
Free vote, free choice.
Free thoughts, free words.
Free from fears.
Let free words loose
Between your ears.

Hear free words, hear free words.
Come and hear free words here.

TOBRUK 21ST JUNE 1942

Waiting:
Smithy pulls two Woodbines from the pack
cups his hands to light them,
passes one over.
Then from his battledress jacket,
takes the half empty packet
and tosses it to me
"I won't be needing these where I'm going".

After:
I hear Smithy
calling out my name.
I spin round to look for him
amongst the thousands of prisoners,
as we are herded together.
"Be cool, be calm, and be collected"
a voice nearby says quietly.

Later:
I am told he caught it as the battle began,
an Iti machine gun,
as he jumped down from the back of the Leyland.
Cut in half before he reached the ground.

Now:
I wipe my cheek
with the side of my thumb,
take a drag on a Woodbine,
watch it glow red in the dark.

SONNET WRITTEN IN A CITY CEMETERY

A great green grass radula stretches vast
before me, its hundreds of marble teeth
stand gleaming in the sun while beneath,
the shells of antique hopes and visions rest,
ingested by the creeping soil.
Over years, rain and tears wash the faded trail
of careworn ifs and buts, man's muddy soles
leave to make his mark upon this world.

As future generations come and go
and dream their dreams of immortality
(place each faltering footstep in the snow)
attach their hopes to temporary tracks,
so time and nature bury all below
and sun and wind and rain erase all marks.

PUMA

There is a Puma
at large in the city.
One or two people
have claimed to see its shadow,
like that of a large cat.

The only substantial evidence:
piss puddles in alleyways
and the dismembered corpses
of several
Kentucky fried chickens.

THE LAST HOUSE

The last house
in a demolished street,

standing alone and empty;
as you, childlike,

throw stones
at my windows.

THE BIRD

Don't come in bird
she said
as the afternoon sun shone
through the open window
and seeing her upon the bed
i reached out to touch her
then stopped
fearing that in the moment of contact
that which i was reaching for
would be misunderstood
and in fright might
fly out of the window
and mistaking it for a bird
she would not let it in again.

SUMMER STORM

You arrived swiftly
a cloudburst
out of the blue
      sky suddenly
filled with rain
        drops cool
refreshing.

Then the THUNDER
Ominous
rumbling.
Storm clouds
  without silver linings.

You passed swiftly
a summer storm
     leaving me cold
          wet
        alone
         blue
sky empty
except for a rainbow
     without
        colour.

TRUE LIFE CONFESSIONS

He grabbed love with both hands
but holding it too tightly,
strangled it.

He cut up the memories
that bound it to his heart,
then wandered the city

disposing the burnt and charred
remnants in old carrier bags
and emptied lager cans.

He covered the kisses
in cement and threw them
one by one into the river.

Eventually
he sat down
in front of a typewriter,

made a statement
signed:
True Life Confessions.

FRACTALS

They are still there,
the bruises
my father gave me.
The tattoo of repeated patterns:
the broken window frames of his belt buckle,
the blue moons of his half sovereign signet ring.

Over the years
they have faded from my skin,
yellowing
like memory,
like the photograph of dad,
regulation moustache and peaked cap,
standing to attention
with his broom and corporation dustcart.

From time to time,
from the corner of my eye
I still catch glances
of the black and blue,
against the pink flesh
of my children.

AND STILL THE WORD HUNG IN MID AIR

And still the word hung in mid air,
chill net curtain blown between us
emotional crowbar wrought from where
and if and how and was and as.
And flew the wind in face of reason
as dark the time grew with the season
now near is end, speak truth is treason.

And still the word hung in mid air,
looked on and laughed as
shallowness drowned deep despair,
doubting ivy slipped crack to crack
grew here to then and then to back.
Consequences slipstreamed actions
released the howl of chained reaction.

And still the word hung in mid air,
stared eye to eye
close as fist, far from care
once danced in time, owed to joy
now out of space, in the void
applied the brakes, supplied the friction
as into every once and which way
flew the inevitable contradiction.

THE POSTER

A poster on a wall.
Colours faded
by sun and rain
and time.

For a film that I once saw
with someone I once knew.

A plot that I can't quite remember.
A face that I can't quite recall.

A memory on a wall.
Colours faded
by sun and rain
and time.

SOME CHANGE PLEASE?

Street tanned
hand
stretches from its tepee.

Can ya spare uz some change?

Street wise
eyes
stare unexpectant.

Ha ya gut any spare change?

The obligatory dog
sleeps,
oblivious to all.

Spare uz some change please?

The obligatory Special Brew can
stands,
oblivion to one.

Any change? Please.

Ya Bastards!

DEEP END

In slurried, mild, luke cold winter.
Immured by her hard earned home,
childless, dreamless, long-term spinster,
needle-points life's slow slipped splinter,
chases the hard shard to the bone.
Places a glass, front and centre,
with gin & tonic brimming full,
plumbs old depths in her swimming pool.

Sips the spring when she was younger,
careering against the current,
mouth and eyes closed to the moment,
missed the world, floating by her.
Now sits and with her broken glass,
unpicks the stitches of her past.

ARROWS

There is an apple
on my head
and for sometime,
someone or something
has been firing arrows at it.

Due largely to general inaccuracy
most have missed
both
the apple and myself,
a few have caused
minor flesh wounds
and one
or two
have pierced my heart.

ON THE ROCKS

Hot sunlight sparkles across the Serpentine,
echoing in the bursting bubbles
it catch lights in our Cokes;
contrasted by the dull glint of the ice cubes.

Your words sail, windborne
on the slow grassy air,
they float gently,
over the white plastic glare
of the Plantery Bar table,
"This is beautiful, I could stay here all day".

Ice clinks in your glass.
I bask in your presence,
blissfully unaware of the titanic finality
of this afternoon,
of what lies hidden behind your sunglasses.

GAULOISES

and smoke
        was promises
words
      come through unbid
stoke faded
        blue memory,
dreams end
      unchallenged.

SKRYING

If I stare long enough into the polished black obsidian mirror,
they will come to me
the angels or demons.

If I look deep enough into the crystal orb
or focus meditation on a stone.

If I stay awake for nights on end
or work out till I drop.

If I drink enough red biddy
or lick slime from a toad's back.

If I fry up magic mushrooms
or chase the dragons tail.

If I fill my lungs from a bag of glue
or pull a noose tight round my neck until all air is gone.

If I look too long into your eyes,
they will come to me
the angels or demons.

ILLUSION

The saying goes:
the swiftness of the hand deceives the eye
- but that's a lie.

It's words that deceive,
misdirect
and wave their wand.

The magician's art
is dark indeed
as he gently leads
you up the unguarded path,
to reveal -
what you will
believe.

He has no magic,
just one trick,
to tell a tale and tell it well.

Words alone will spin a spell,
steer you
to a wrong conclusion.

Conjuror,
poet,
priest
and politician,
each performs their own illusion.

SOMETHING IN HER EYES

A child
bedraggled
something in her eyes,
knowledge
(beyond despair),
experience
(deeper than the soul).

A child
something
in her bedraggled eyes,
experience
(beyond knowledge).
Soul
(deeper than despair).

A child
knowledge
in her experienced eyes,
something (despair).
Soul bedraggled
(deeper than beyond).

THE ROAD TO TIANANMEN SQUARE

Out of the corridors of power
the order rumbled.
The People's Army marched.

"Go back, you are not needed here"
the People cried
"Long live the People's heroes".

This time they did not stop.
We heard the vicious mongrel bark,
saw the dragon's flame.

Could not believe until
the people divided;
rivers flowed red in the gutter.

SHOCK HORROR PROBE

The British designer:
Proud of his design skills.
Proud of his technical abilities.
Admires the good, strong British workmanship.
Compact lightweight and packs a real punch,
he has made a good job of this one.

The Chinese soldier:
Proud of his uniform, his rank.
Proud of his skills and technique,
learnt and honed during his four years
in the Tibet Autonomous Region
he will make a good job of this one.

The Tibetan Nun:
Proud of her religion, country, culture.
Proud of her voice, her songs,
sung in the long dark prison nights.
"Through the compassion of the all knowing one
*Peace will prevail in Tibet"**

Naked, curled foetal, hugging
a tear-streaked wall, paralysed
by fear and pain.
Days later, mouth and vagina,
still reeling from the aftershocks.
Imprisoned beneath
her blistered tongue,
a scream that can not escape.

"We Will Never be Disheartened"
- Nun's Song, Drapchi Prison.

ECLIPSED AGAIN

Even at the point of totality,
when the moon
for one triumphant moment is
no longer bathed in reflected glory.
Even then,
all any one
can talk of is the sun.

MOON SHADOW

Moon shadow dances.
The black circle of her day into night
skirt spins out.

Moon shadow dances.
Her diamonds and beads sparkle
at this brief flirtation.

Moon shadow dances.
Birds cease their song, the atmosphere
is pregnant with unseen messages.

Moon shadow dances.
Age old traveller,
her gypsy-soled feet carry her on.

CORNISH GIANTS

They beckon, white arms waving
across Bodmin Moor.
Curious, quixotic, I am drawn
towards them, full tilt

Immense pagan priests
describing symbolic circles.
Silently praying to nature
for power,
a mere echo of her own.

ONCE UPON A WITCHING TIME

Once upon a witching time
you put a spell on me,
serpentined around my heart
daisy-chained it to a tree.

Frozen by a potion,
hemlocked within your eyes.
Chosen by emotions,
wherein the magic lies.

With the darkening of the wild woods
around the sacred grove
and the howling of the wild wolves,
my uneasiness did grow.

Many and long, the years have past
since last you walked this way.
Yet in the sacred grove
a gnarled and ancient oak,
does in the wild wind sway.

PREY

Hovering hawk-like;
stone-still and talon-sharp.

High

above my heart.

Shivering, shaking,
stopped in my tracks.
Petrified by your piercing eyes,
held in the strength of your shadow.
Prey
I wait while you

drop

down

from

the

sky

to tear, my life to shreds.

GROSS INDECENCIES

By the gloom grey unsterile light
of the station lavatory,
in front of an off-white adamant urinal.
A grey-haired pinstriped city gent
masturbates rhythmically
his eyes riveted
on the young, black and obviously
                                        gifted penis
of a West Indian rent boy
who gyrates his hips slowly
to the bluesy back beat of a five pound note
and lends a helping hand to speed
the proceedings:
cautiously glancing toward the
lavatory entrance.
Unnoticed by the other men around them
who are
engrossed in their own indecencies.

FREEZING POINT

Pavement
wet with :
"It's cold enough to…"
but this is ...

Kerbstone
glistens :
"Clouds look like…"
but it won't :

Sleeping bag huddles in a doorway.
"It's cold enough to…"
but this is ...
"Clouds look like…"
but it won't :

Dog barks.
Sleeping bag
huddles in a doorway.
"It's cold enough to…"
but this is …

Rain falls.
Dog licks
a white hand,
but it won't .

"It's cold enough to …"
but this is London.

MEASURING THE VOLUME OF AN ELEPHANT

A thousand people
     walk in different directions.

Metal boxes contain
     repeated images,
     repeated images
on a glass canvas.

A million people,
paid to move numbers,
   move numbers
       around.

A child disguised,
   disguised as a skeleton.

Dies with flies on his eyes
   and nothing,
nothing in his distended stomach
but the truth

   the truth.

THE FLOWER GARDEN

Mother grips tightly
a bunch of fresh cut flowers,
as she walks surely
between the white stones.

I struggle behind
carrying with two hands
a large grey metal watering can,
water slops over the top.

The remains of last week's flowers
are carefully removed.
I wrinkle my nose,
empty reeking liquid
from a cold metal vase,
cleanse and refill.

Mum arranges the new flowers lovingly,
tends to the minute walled garden around them.
She looks up
"Don't play on the humps in the grass dear"

In the ordinariness of this routine,
two things puzzle me:
why is this book
(whose black letters pose
mysteriously on the open page)
made of stone
and why does Michael
want to sleep here?

WHAT A WASTE
(for Ian Dury)

There's a feeling, like the memory of a Kursaal ride,
an old wind, a cold wind that stirs inside.
Rolling in like the wind off the estuary tide,
down a dead flat, mud flat, eight miles wide.

And
somewhere, somefing, somehow sighed,
what a waste - what a waste,
Ian Dury died.

Snazzy little geezer wiv a spazzy stick.
A concrete mixer voice, rough and fick.
Takes the stage, like a fief on the nick.
Hard bard, art tart, don't giva shit.

And
somefing, somehow, somewhere sighed,
what a waste - what a waste,
Ian Dury died.

Words of an angel, dressed wiv a mallet,
mixed wiv spit from a painters palette.
Raw sound, foot down, pushed to the limit,
escaped from the cage of an old cock linnet.

And
somehow, somewhere, somefing sighed,
what a waste - what a waste,
Ian Dury died.

PUTTING THE BOOKS STRAIGHT

In her annual report,
the head Librarian had written
"Julie is neat and methodical,
but needs to interact with the public more."
Now she puts every tenth book away
in the wrong place
and spends much more time helping the readers.

THE RAGU

The pasta water is beginning to boil
and I am working up a sweat
dancing round the kitchen
to an old rock 'n' roll song on Radio 2.
Charlotte enters,
stands at the door
teen eyes stare at me, until
I stop dancing;
she goes to the fridge
takes out a carton,
pours juice into a glass,
she sips at the blackberry,
flashes her eyes
briefly in my direction,
turns like a toreador
and leaves
without a word.
Jerry Lee has finished singing.
I pick up a wooden spoon,
slowly stir
the simmering ragu.

GRAFFITI

I used to carve our initials in the bark of trees,
aerosol brickwork with my
LUV 4 U.
Posters and railway carriages
carried heartfelt messages
scrawled in black felt tip.

Yesterday:
I found a strange paintbrush
in the bathroom.

Today:
Suspicious, I search your handbag,
I find bleaches, solvents and
scrubbing brushes.

Tomorrow:
The writing is on the wall.

PHANTOMS

Joseph lost two and a half fingers
to a buzz saw
and a wife to bowel cancer.

"It's funny, you know," he said,
about the fingers
"I can still feel'em there,

It is only when
I need to hold something
that I feel the loss."

THE APPLE

I took an apple
from under the tree
this morning.

Still wet with
dew
from the grass

and ate it
on the way
to work,

bitter and sharp
it brought tears
to my tongue.

6.55 a.m. RAYLEIGH STATION.

Between the platforms,
between the rails,
on the rust dusted stones
between the sleepers.
Lies a lager can,
bright green when it landed
last summer, abandoned by
some unsteady late night traveller.

Six months accumulated dirt
has turned green to grey,
red rust spreads slowly
from its crumpled centre,
blood oozing from an old wound.

In the winter half and half light,
as the station fluorescents try
vainly to outshine the dawn sky.
Among the remnants of darkness
that cling to the sleepers,
my eyes pick out the cans shape;
its edges etched with white frost.
Nature's palette reveals
art beyond imagination or technique.

COLLECTOR

I lie in a box
at the bottom of a hole,
a Picasso-faced woman
leans over (the eye
between her breasts,
unblinking),
throws down
a handful of skinned cats.

Meanwhile:
a magpie with a halo
lands on my chest,
asks for my 1st class ticket.
I search, seemingly forever,
eventually produce a piece
of crumpled green cardboard,
by now the bird is a skeleton and
beetles have collected in my pockets.

DREAMSCAPE

A farmhand dreams
some much-tilled field's
    distant blue horizon.

    Nightly this road
was another child's
latent rambling journey.

AUTUMN LEAVES ME COLD

The close, hot
tempered days of summer
have departed.

Autumn has arrived
with thick morning mists
that obscure my vision.

I cannot see
      that the leaves
             are
falling

only their beauty
against a sky
      grey as your eyes.

And you
      like the evenings
      have grown colder.

BAREFOOT

Barefoot we tiptoe
carefully
through the broken crockery.
Thrown at each other
across the void
that lies between us.

Still close
enough to hurt each other,
too far apart to care.

As we tiptoe
barefoot
through the broken crockery.
Carefully avoiding
the lies between us.

ARTIFICIAL FLAVOURINGS

Inside my skull
there is a monkfish steak.
Its succulent white flesh
has no strong taste of its own.
So I flavour it with sauces.

Sauces seasoned with strong images,
fading sounds, lasting aromas,
hot spicy moments, salty tears,
a splash of intoxication, some bitter memories
and a few crushed hopes.

CLEARING

I thought I'd said goodbye,
with a single red rose
and a handful of earth.

Now I'm doing it again,
packing you into black plastic bags
divided between
Sue Ryder's and the dump.

As you slip through my fingers
and the faint smell
of Chanel No.19 blurs my eyes,

at the back of the wardrobe
or tucked in a drawer,
I am surprised to find you:
someone else.

RUNNING ON AIR

I'm running on air,
there's nothing left
and I no longer care.
I had a tank full, a brim full, a skin full,
much more than my share,
but its no longer there.
I'm empty inside.
I'm running on air.

Helter skelter through life
on a white knuckle ride.
Nowhere to shelter,
nowhere to hide.
Caught in a race that's no longer fair.
I've lost my shell and life is a hare.
I'm out on a limb.
I'm running on air,
there's nothing left
and I no longer care.

Pursued by an avalanche.
A runaway sledge,
I've run out of rope,
I can see the cliff edge.
I reach out for something
but there's nothing there,
My hand comes back empty.
I'm running on air.

I saw the world laid at my feet,
now my soul's been flayed bare.
The rugs been pulled from under me,
all I can do is stare.
There is nothing where the ground should be.
I've nothing left to stand on.
I'm running on air.

REMEMBER, REMEMBER...

That was some bonfire we had,
its tall flames licking and spitting
at the dark sky.
The intense heat made your cheek glow,
even when you had turned away,
and singed the hairs on the back of my hands
when I tried to hook out
the foil wrapped potatoes with a rake.

Today on the frost-dusted lawn
there is a circle of white ash;
picking up the same rake
by its burnt black handle.
I scrape away the surface to expose,
embers still too hot to shovel away.

APPARITION

It's late Sunday night
and we're driving back to Essex,
through Thetford Forest
on the A134.

The road is empty
apart from the occasional
flash of headlamps
speeding in the opposite direction.

Beyond the full-beam
and in the rear-view mirror, darkness.
To the side, away from the road
a soft curtain of trees,

suddenly, red eyed
among the bramble and ferns -
a Muntjac, white,
dressed in the headlight's glare.

HISTORIAN'S GUIDE TO THE GALAXY

Brought into being
with a cosmic slap on the bottom.
Consigned to oblivion
by the blown fuse
of an imploding star.
In between,
nothing of consequence,
the weather was changeable,
the butterflies,
beautiful.